Fish Culture, by Charles Edward Walker

Title: Amateur Fish Culture

Author: Charles Edward Walker

Release Date: February 29, 2008 [EBook #24719]

Language: English

Character set encoding: ISO-8859-1

AMATEUR FISH CULTURE

BY CHARLES EDWARD WALKER

AUTHOR OF "OLD FLIES IN NEW DRESSES" "SHOOTING ON
A SMALL INCOME," ETC

WESTMINSTER ARCHIBALD CONSTABLE & CO LTD 2
WHITEHALL GARDENS

1901

Butler & Tanner, The Selwood Printing Works, Frome, and
London.

PREFACE

My aim, in this little book, has been to give information and hints
which will prove useful to the amateur. Some of the plans and
apparatus suggested would not be suitable for fish culture on a
large scale, but my object has been to confine myself entirely to
operations on a small scale. I have to thank the Editor of *Land
and Water* for permission to publish in book form what first
appeared as a series of articles.

CHARLES WALKER.

Mayfield, Sussex. *March, 1901.*

CONTENTS

CHAPTER PAGE

CHAPTER I

INTRODUCTORY

Fish culture of a certain kind dates from very early times, but its scientific development has only come about quite recently. Most people know that in our own country the monks had stew ponds, where they kept fish, principally carp, and also that the Romans kept fish in ponds. In the latter case we hear more often of the eel than of other fish. The breeding of trout and salmon, and the artificial spawning and hatching of ova, are, however, an innovation of our own time.

Much has been discovered about the procreation of fish, and in no case have scientists worked so hard and discovered more than in the case of *Salmonidæ*. Fish culture, particularly trout culture, has become a trade, and a paying one. To any one who has the least idea of the difficulties to be overcome in rearing *Salmonidæ*, this fact alone proves that fish culture must have progressed to a very advanced stage as a science.

This advance has in very many, if not in the majority of cases, been made by the bitter experience gained through failures and mishaps, for these have led fish culturists to try many different means to prevent mischances, or to rectify them if they have happened. Some of the most serious difficulties experienced by the early fish culturists who bred *Salmonidæ* can now be almost disregarded, for they hardly exist for the modern fish culturist, with the knowledge he possesses of the experience of others.

So much of what has been done in fish culture is generally known to those who have studied and practised it, that the beginner can nowadays commence far ahead of the point whence the first fish culturists started. Many of his difficulties have been overcome for him already, and though he will not, of course, meet with the success of the man of experience, still he ought with the exercise of an average amount of intelligence to avoid such failures as would completely disgust him.

There are many pieces of water containing nothing but coarse fish which are very suitable for trout of some kind. Ponds, particularly those which have a stream running through them, will, as a rule, support a good head of trout if properly managed. Again a water which contains trout may become more or less depleted, and here it is necessary to supply the deficiency of trout by some means. The easiest way is, of course, to buy yearling or two-year-old fish from a piscicultural establishment, of which there are many in the kingdom, but I know that there are many fishermen who would much prefer to rear their own fish from the ova, than to buy ready-made fish. Any one who has the time and opportunity to rear his own fish will be amply repaid by the amusement and interest gained, and it should be the cheaper method of stocking or re-stocking a water.

The same remarks apply to a certain extent to waters which will not support trout, or where the owner wants more coarse fish. The stock of coarse fish may be improved by fish culture just as much as a stock of trout.

In his first year or two, it is very possible that the amateur will not save very much by being his own pisciculturist. If, however, he is careful, and works with intelligence, it is quite possible that he may succeed better than he had hoped and rear a good head of fish at a less cost than the purchase of yearlings. In any case he will have had a great deal of pleasure and gained experience as well as reared some fish.

In the present little volume, I propose to try and deal with fish culture in such a way as to help the amateur who wishes to rear fish to stock his own water. Much of the existing literature of the subject deals with it on such a large scale that the amateur is frightened to attempt what is apparently so huge an undertaking.

Fish culture may, however, be carried out on a small scale with success, and though considerable attention is necessary, particularly with young *Salmonidæ*, it is not a task which involves a very great proportion of the time of any one undertaking it. It is absolutely necessary, however, that the amateur fish culturist should live on the spot, or have some one who is intelligent and perfectly trustworthy who does. In every case in my experience, trusting the care of young fish to a keeper or servant has resulted in failure, and in every failure I have seen where the fish have not been trusted to the care of a servant, the cause has been very obvious, and could easily have been avoided.

The rearing of trout is the most important branch of fish culture to the amateur, and fortunately but slight modifications are necessary in rearing other fish. What is good enough for trout is good enough for most fish, therefore I think that I shall be right in describing trout culture at considerable length, and dealing with other fish in a somewhat summary manner. The difference in the management, etc., of other fish I shall point out after describing how to rear trout.

To begin with, the amateur must not suppose that because he puts fish into a stream or pond he will succeed in stocking that water or increasing the head of fish. There are many other things to be considered. The river, stream, or pond must be of a suitable character for the fish, and there must be plenty of food. I am sure that it is much more important to consider carefully whether the water is suitable, and contains a proper supply of food, than to consider how the fish are to be obtained, for recourse may always be had to a professional fish culturist--fish of almost any kind and any age can be bought ready made.

The point I would impress upon the amateur more forcibly than anything else, is that he should be sure that there is plenty for his fish to eat in the water, before he thinks of putting them into it. It is for this reason that I devote my next chapter chiefly to the stocking of waters with food and to the improvement of the food supply in waters where some food already exists.

CHAPTER II

STOCKING WATERS WITH FOOD

It may seem somewhat superfluous to say that fish cannot live in any water unless that water contains the food supply necessary for them to thrive upon, and yet this is the point most often overlooked in stocking waters with fish. Small attempts at stocking with creatures suitable for food, particularly after the fish have been already introduced, are not at all likely to succeed. Such an important matter when treated as a small afterthought is almost sure to end in failure of the whole business of stocking.

But a small amount of thought will convince any one that in order that there may be a sufficient amount of animal life in a water, there must be an adequate vegetable life, for weeds are almost always necessary to the well-being of the creatures which serve as food for fishes.

In the case of a pond it is generally fairly easy to introduce a good stock of suitable weeds. The best method is to let the pond down as low as possible, and then to plant some weeds round the margin; the water is then allowed to gradually fill up the pond, and as it rises weeds are planted round the rising margin of the water. In ponds which cannot be emptied at all, or not sufficiently to carry out this plan, weeds may be planted in an easy but not quite so effectual a manner. They may be planted in shallow baskets containing some mud from the bottom of the pond, and then lowered in suitable places from a boat, or bundles of the weed may be tied to stones and dropped into the water in a similar manner.

These latter methods are, of course, not so good as actually planting the weeds round the advancing margin of the water, for success depends to a certain extent upon chance. Some of the weeds thus planted are, however, sure to take root and grow.

Plants of different kinds, of course, are necessary at different depths and on different kinds of bottoms, and good kinds are necessary at the margin of the water as well. I give a list of some suitable plants of each kind at the end of this chapter.

Similar methods are used in planting weeds in rivers and streams to those used in ponds. If the weeds are planted in baskets, the baskets must, of course, be weighted when put in a position where the current can act upon them.

Besides vegetation in the water, vegetation on the bank is of considerable importance. I shall deal with this at a later period more fully, as trees and bushes, besides harbouring many insects which serve as food for fish, have also considerable importance in giving cover to the fish and to the fisherman who is pursuing them.

I think that in the case of a bare water, a year at least should be devoted to developing a good supply of vegetation. This will generally produce a considerable amount of animal life, without any artificial help, but judicious help will be sure to accelerate matters to a considerable extent. I would, however, advise the amateur not to attempt to introduce a quantity of creatures into his water, until the vegetable life therein is well established. For instance, though fresh-water snails are desirable in every trout water, if introduced in large numbers into a water in which the vegetation is small and not well established, they will eat down the weeds too much and then die off from disease caused by want of sufficient nourishment.

Having established the vegetable life well in a water, and developed it to a considerable extent, the amateur may begin to examine his water, and find out how much animal life exists there, and to stock with creatures suitable for food, according to what he finds in the water.

Fresh-water snails are always desirable. In streams, or in ponds with streams running into them, the fresh-water shrimps (*Gammarus pulex*) should always be tried. It does not do in some waters, but where it does thrive it increases very rapidly, and forms about the best article of food that can be given to trout. *Corixæ*, which thrive in ponds and sluggish waters, should always be introduced. They increase rapidly, and are taken by most fish, particularly by trout. The amateur should be careful when he introduces these creatures to make sure that he is putting in the right creature. The water-boatman (*Nautonecta glauca*) is a member of the same family, but is no use as food for the fish. He swims on his back, is longer and narrower than are *Corixæ*, which do not swim on their backs, are smaller, broader, and live much more under water than the water-boatman. It is generally advisable to avoid water-beetles, as most of them are more likely to do harm than good, such a number of our water-beetles being carnivorous. They will probably not harm adult fish, but they will destroy ova and fry. I have known a *Dytiscus marginalis* kill a trout of nearly a quarter of a pound in weight.

In order to make sure of not introducing carnivorous water-beetles into a water, I think it best as a rule not to introduce beetles at all. *Corixæ* are, however, so like beetles, that many people call them beetles, and therefore I will give a few points which will make them easily distinguishable from each other. In beetles, the wing-cases (elytra) meet exactly in the middle line, in *Corixæ* and other water-bugs, the anterior wings, which resemble the elytra of beetles, overlap, which causes the line on the back to curve away to one side at the lower end. In beetles the wings which lie under the wing-cases are folded up on themselves, and when spread out are much larger than the wing-cases. The wings are transparent and very delicate. In *Corixæ* the posterior wings, which lie under the hard and horny anterior wings, are a little shorter than the anterior wings; they are not folded up on themselves and are not so delicate and transparent as the wings of the beetle.

Such small creatures as *Daphnia pulex*, *Cyclops quadricornis* and *Rotifera* should be introduced into ponds.

Snails (*Gasteropoda*) may be roughly divided into three classes, according to the shape of their shells: (1) Flat-shaped coils (type *Planorbis corneus*); (2) Oblong-shaped, somewhat like a trumpet (type *Limnæa stagnalis*); and (3) Ear-shaped (type *Limnæa auricularia*). *Limnæa auricularia* is particularly suitable for deep waters, and *L. pereger*, whose shell is of type 2, is a most valuable addition to the food supply in any fish pond. It is one of the commonest of our fresh-water snails.

Mussels (*Conchifera*) are another valuable article of food. There are a great many different kinds, and the larger ones should, as a rule, be avoided. *Sphæriidæ* and *Pisidia* are probably the best.

In many cases it is advisable to attempt the introduction of some flies which are not present. There are several cases in which the May-fly has been successfully introduced, and also the Grannom. Small *Ephemeridæ* seem to me preferable to any other flies.

With regard to suitable plants for comparatively deep water in ponds or lakes, lakewort and stonewort grow on the bottom, and do not, as a rule, attain any considerable height. White and yellow water-lilies also grow in fairly deep water; the water-lobelia is also an excellent plant for ponds.

In streams some of the best plants are water-crowfoot, water-starwort, and the great water moss. Anacharis should not be introduced into any water, either pond or stream, unless it can be kept down easily. It will otherwise become an unmitigated nuisance.

Marginal plants are a very important consideration, and plenty of them should be grown. Water-celery and water-cress are perhaps the best food-producing marginal plants that can be grown. Bullrushes and brooklime are also good, but the bullrushes must be planted judiciously.

CHAPTER III

SUITABLE FISH AND SUITABLE WATERS

Having stocked his water with suitable vegetation and food, the next matter which should engage the attention of the amateur, is what fish he had better introduce. He should, where there is a fair chance of success, introduce a trout of some sort, as they give better sport than coarse fish.

The introduction of salmon into a river is not likely to be attempted by the amateur, but the head of salmon frequenting a river is undoubtedly affected in the most marvellous manner by artificial means. In Canada and the United States this is particularly remarkable, but the operations are conducted on a gigantic scale.

In the case of a stream or river where brown trout already exist, or have recently existed, in fair numbers, re-stock with these fish, for they can hardly be bettered in our waters. There are, however, some sluggish rivers where brown trout do not thrive when they are introduced. In such rivers and in many ponds in the South of England I believe that no better fish exists than the rainbow trout. I say particularly in the south, because I do not think that the rainbow trout will ever really thrive and breed in cold waters. I have at other times given numerous examples which go to show that the rainbow will only thrive in warm waters.[1] I will therefore only quote the case of New Zealand. The rainbow trout was introduced into both islands, but while it thrived amazingly in the warm waters of the North Island, it has proved a comparative failure in the cold waters of the South Island.

[1] *The Rainbow Trout.* Lawrence & Bullen, London.

While the common or brown trout (*Salmo fario*) and the rainbow trout (*Salmo irideus*) are, in my opinion, to be strongly encouraged in the waters suitable to their respective qualities, the American brook trout (*Salvelinus fontinalis*) does not seem to have met with the approval of most of the authorities on pisciculture in this country. My experience of this fish is not sufficient for my holding any very strong views with regard to its suitability to British waters. In one case I know that it was a great success for two seasons, but I have not had any opportunity of following it up in this particular instance. In another case it was a decided failure. I am sure that it should not be introduced into streams where brown trout thrive, and I am doubtful of its ever succeeding in waters which are suitable to the rainbow trout.

Of all the trout, the rainbow is the hardiest, and the one with which the amateur pisciculturist is most likely to be successful. It is also the fish most likely to supply a want felt by very many fishermen, a good sporting fish in waters where the common trout will not thrive.

In large and deep ponds with a good stream, or in lakes, char may be tried with a prospect of success. They require cold waters, and I have never heard of their being successfully introduced in the South of England. They are a more difficult fish to rear than trout.

Grayling have many violent opponents, but I am inclined to think that they do but little if any harm in a trout stream, and they supply excellent fishing during part of the close season for trout. They seem to thrive best in chalk streams, but there are no doubt many waters which would carry a good head of grayling which at present contain only trout. They probably do much less harm than most of the coarse fish constantly found in trout streams. The great crime attributed to them is that they eat the spawn of the trout, but I am inclined to think that the harm they do in this way is much over estimated. They spawn at a different time and would not be likely to frequent the spawning places at the same time as the trout. I have no doubt that an infinitely greater proportion of trout ova are eaten by the trout themselves than by grayling in rivers which contain both fish. Chalk streams and those rivers with gravelly bottoms and with alternate shallows and pools seem to be the most suited to the grayling.

Among coarse fish the rudd is one of the best from the fly-fisher's point of view. It takes the fly readily, is very prolific and very easy to introduce. It thrives remarkably well in ponds which contain a good supply of food. Its fry serve as excellent food for other fish, particularly trout, but I have known cases where it increased rapidly in a pond at the expense of the trout. It can, however, be kept under by judicious netting.

The dace is another fish which gives sport to the fly-fisherman. It will not thrive in ponds. In some rivers, however, where trout--brown trout, at any rate--will not thrive, the dace does very well. In the case of the Sussex Ouse this is most remarkable. Little more than ten years ago there were no dace in that river, now it swarms with them. Their presence is attributed to the fact that some dace, brought there as live-baits for pike, escaped destruction and established the present stock. Sluggish and muddy rivers seem to produce the best dace. Chubb, which also possess many points to recommend them to the fisherman, will also do well in such rivers.

To those who enjoy bottom fishing and possess a pond, even a small one, I can recommend no fish more highly than the king-carp. It is a much bolder-feeding and gamer fish than the common carp, and is just as easy to introduce. While dealing with carp I may mention that the goldfish, when introduced into a suitable pond, grows to a very large size. I have caught them over a pound in weight.

The perch is a very prolific fish, and will thrive in ponds with a very small stream running into them, and in sluggish rivers. Other coarse fish are as a rule easy to introduce into a water. Though perch fry form excellent food for trout, perch, and of course pike, should be kept out of a trout water.

The suitability of a water depends to a great extent (as to its capacity of supporting a healthy stock of fish) upon its having plenty of suitable vegetation upon the banks. Therefore if the banks are bare of vegetation, willows and alders, as being quick growing and easily established trees, should be freely planted upon the banks. This fortunately is very easily done, for willow and alder sticks cut and put into the ground in the spring are pretty sure to do well. It is needless to say that the moister spots should be chosen for the willows, though they will do well in suitable soil in comparatively dry places. Besides giving shade and shelter to the fish, which is always an important consideration, a considerable quantity of food is bred upon trees and shrubs at the water side. I have found as many as eighteen caterpillars in the stomach of a trout which I caught under an overhanging oak tree.

CHAPTER IV

TROUT. PRELIMINARY HINTS AND ADVICE

The amateur who is beginning trout culture had better by all means buy eyed ova from a fish cultural establishment. There are many of these in the British Isles, and nowadays eyed ova are packed and sent safely all over the country. The artificial spawning of trout is not an undertaking in which the beginner is likely to achieve great success, and therefore I should advise him to avoid relying upon it when he commences his operations as a fish culturist.

Collecting the ova of wild trout is also an operation of some difficulty, and lays the beginner open to much more disappointment than if he deals with eyed ova purchased from a reliable establishment. Instead of having to watch and care for the ova through a critical and dangerous period, he receives them shortly before the young fish hatch out, when the ova are not in the most delicate stage.

It is of the greatest importance that everything should be ready for the ova long before they are expected, as hurry and new apparatus are likely to cause failure. Any concrete and varnished or enamelled woodwork should be exposed to the action of a current of water for at least five or six weeks before they are brought into actual use.

The choice of a suitable spot in which to make his hatchery is a serious point for the consideration of the amateur. A spring is the best water supply as a rule, for the water is usually of a fairly even temperature, and does not require filtering, but water from a stream where trout are known to live is quite safe. A few years ago it would have been necessary for any one wishing to take up fish culture, to erect a building in which to place his hatchery if he intended to hatch any number of eggs, in order to guard against frosts. At the present time, the eyed ova of even the brown trout (*Salmo fario*) can be obtained sufficiently late to be safe against a frost severe enough to cause any damage, and as the rainbow trout (*Salmo irideus*) spawns in February and March, the amateur is, at the time he receives the eyed ova, quite safe from frost.

The best method to pursue is to make long narrow ponds, with a current running through them, and to hatch the eggs out in trays and boxes suspended in these ponds. When the young fish hatch out, the trays which contained the ova can be removed, and the young fish kept in the boxes. Later on the young fish can be released from the boxes into the ponds. I shall subsequently describe how these ponds, trays, and boxes should be made.

The rearing ponds should be made, if possible, at a fall in the level of the water supply, so that they may be easily emptied. This is an important point which is frequently overlooked by amateurs. There should be an outlet on a level with the bottom of the pond, and if the water escapes through a pipe, that pipe should incline downwards. This, in a series of ponds, of course necessitates the ponds being at different levels, but the water is thus under much better control than if the outlet is at a higher level, and the ponds are easily emptied. Ponds may, however, be worked successfully with the outlet in mid-water, or even near the surface, though this does not ensure such a certainty of change of water throughout the pond. It is not, however, always possible to obtain such a difference in level between the supply and waste. In such cases the ponds should be made shallower near the outlet.

A popular idea seems to be that a gravel bottom is necessary for the well-being of trout; this is quite a mistake. Personally, I believe that a good earth bottom is best in a rearing pond, and even in a pond lined with concrete I should always put a layer of mould, preferably turf mould, at the bottom. With the use of this mould during the subsequent operations in rearing trout I shall deal later on.

The size of the ponds, of course, depends upon the number of trout to be reared. It is better to have several medium sized ponds than one large one, as then accident or disease occurring in a pond will only affect a portion of the stock of fish. Mr. J. J. Armistead in *An Angler's Paradise, and How to Obtain It*, says: "A pond sixty feet long, four feet wide, and about three feet deep, will hold ten or fifteen thousand fry at first, and give them plenty of room to grow, but by the end of July the number should be reduced to five thousand, which may be left till October, when they should again be thinned out, or, better still, put into larger pond."

I should advise the amateur who is dealing with only a few thousand fish to work on a smaller scale in these proportions, and to make these changes gradually, and yet more gradually as the season advances. That is to say, work with a third of the number of fry in ponds half the size and move some fish several times before the end of July. As October approaches, make changes of smaller numbers of fish more frequently.

Late in the autumn is, in my opinion, the best time to put the young fish into the water they are to inhabit permanently. It must be a mistake to rear them artificially longer than is necessary, and by the end of November they should be fairly capable of looking after themselves.

Trout, which are artificially reared on chopped meat and other soft foods, suffer from a lack of development in the stomach walls, and also, probably, in the rest of their digestive apparatus. The first case I saw of the stomach of an artificially reared trout was a two-year-old trout, upon which Dr. C. S. Patterson performed an autopsy. The stomach walls were as thin as a sheet of tissue paper. At the time I believed, and, if I remember rightly, he also thought that this was due to atrophy, but I am inclined to think that this idea was only partially correct. The stomach walls of the autumn yearling trout, which is artificially reared on soft food, do not show any marked abnormality in the way of thinness; but as the trout's age increases, so does the thickness of the stomach wall decrease in proportion to its size. This leads me to believe that the development of the stomach wall, at any rate, and probably also of the glands secreting the gastric juice and the digestive apparatus generally, gradually ceases when at about the age of eight or nine months if the trout is fed upon soft food. Probably, also, a certain amount of atrophy and dilatation of the stomach wall is produced. If my observations are correct, so also is the conclusion that a trout which cannot digest hard food, of which a great part of his natural food consists, will not have a really fair chance when turned out. Therefore, I say, turn out your trout in November, unless you can feed them on such food as shrimps, snails, bivalves and *Corixæ*; and if you stock with "ready made" fish, stock with yearlings in the late autumn.

The turning out of his fish in November will also allow the amateur plenty of time to prepare his ponds and apparatus for next year's operations. If the ponds are made on a stream, probably the very best place that can be chosen is where there is a fairly sharp bend in the stream just below a fall. An artificial fall can often be made where the banks are high by damming up the stream several feet. Care must be taken, however, to avoid any risk of the ponds being flooded.

CHAPTER V

TROUT. REARING PONDS, BOXES, AND HATCHING TRAYS

Having decided upon a suitable spot, the amateur must now proceed to make his ponds. Whether he derive his water supply from a spring or from a stream, the amateur had better bring it into his ponds through a pipe. A three-inch pipe will be large enough for a pond thirty feet long, three feet wide, and two feet deep at the deepest part. It is a good thing for the water to fall, some inches at any rate, through the air before it reaches the pond, and in a series of ponds with only one supply, the water should flow through an open trough with stones and other impediments in it, between the ponds. The ponds may be lined entirely with brickwork faced with cement, and in this case the sides should be made perpendicular. The cement should, however, be exposed freely to the action of the running water for a couple of months at least before any ova or fry are introduced.

Another plan, and a simpler and less expensive one, is to face only the ends of the ponds with brick and cement work, carrying the brickwork into the earth on each side, as shown in Fig. 1. In this case the sides of the ponds should be slightly sloped as shown in Figs. 2 and 3. It is advisable if possible to make the outlet at the level of the bottom of the pond, if the pond is lined with cement, but if the pond is only cemented at the ends, it is better to have one in mid-water or even near the surface. As I have said before however, an outlet should be made at the level lowest part of the bottom, so as to facilitate the emptying of the pond. The pond should however be made shallower at the lower end. Fig. 2 shows a section of the upper end, and Fig. 3 of the lower end of such a pond.

[Illustration: Fig. 1.]

[Illustration: Fig. 2.]

[Illustration: Fig. 3.]

The open trough between ponds in a series should be at least three yards in length, but it is better if not straight. Stones and gravel should be put in these troughs in order to make the water as rough as possible, and if some fresh-water shrimps can be introduced so much the better.

If the water is taken from a stream, a leaf screen must be placed at some distance in front of the inlet. This may be made of a hurdle fastened to strong stakes sunk into the bed of the stream. The opening of the inlet should be at least double the size of the sectional area of the pipe through which the water is carried to the ponds, and should be some distance, a couple of feet if possible, below the surface of the water. It is a good thing to put a wire cage over the inlet, and under this a perforated zinc screen is necessary. The inlet from the stream should be so placed that it is easy to get at and clean. The best form of covering for the inlet into the pond I have seen, is a zinc cylinder, the base of which fits over the end of the inlet pipe. The part of this cylinder, which projects 18 inches beyond the pipe, is perforated, as is also the flat end. This can easily be taken off and cleaned, and breaks up the water, making it fall into the pond like a shower bath, causing considerable aeration.

The inlet from the stream should have a trap with which the water may be shut off, as also should the outlet from the pond. When the cylinder on the inlet into the pond is taken off for a minute or so to be cleaned out, both these traps must be closed. This lessens the chance of any creatures likely to do harm getting in during the cleaning. The perforated zinc screen at the inlet from the stream will probably stop any such creatures, but too great care cannot be exercised, and it is always best to be on the safe side.

Movable covers of netting over the ponds are most certainly advisable, particularly if the rearing ponds are in an unfrequented spot near a stream. On one occasion I caught four kingfishers during a period of three weeks, all of which had in some way got under some herring net, which was pegged out carefully over a rearing pond containing trout fry. I never found out how they got in, but once in they were unable to escape.

Ponds such as I have described are of course for the fry when they have reached a certain size, and have already begun to feed well. Other appliances are necessary for hatching out the ova and for the young fish when first hatched. A very good apparatus may be made from a champagne case. This should have large square holes sawn through each end, leaving enough wood to ensure strength and solidity to the box. The box should then have two coats of asphalt varnish, and the square apertures covered with fine perforated zinc. A still better box may be made at a small cost. This consists of a box with a wooden bottom and perforated zinc sides which are supported by a stout wooden frame.

Beyond these boxes all that are required are some perforated zinc hatching trays. These should be 1-1/2 inches deep. They are very easily made, and the ova hatch out well in them. Though ova sometimes hatch out very successfully even when piled up in two or three layers, it is safer to have them in a single layer. The trays should be suspended in the boxes, and the boxes in the ponds close to the inlets, so that a good current of water may flow through them. The bottom of the boxes should be covered with a thick layer of gravel, but the trays are to be used without gravel. It is advisable to have as much grass as possible round the ponds, and such trees as willows and alders should also be planted round them. Willows and alder sticks planted in the early part of the year come into leaf in the same spring, and afford shade to the young fish in the summer. Some suitable weeds should also be grown in the rearing ponds. Water-cress, water-celery, water-lobelia, starwort, and water-milfoil, are all good. They should be arranged, however, so as to prevent as much as possible the little fish finding hiding places, and it is for this reason also that I have recommended slightly sloping banks when the sides of the ponds are not made of cement. The weeds should be planted some time before the little fish are turned out of the boxes.

Finally, I must caution my readers again on one or two points before I leave the subject of the hatching trays, rearing boxes, and ponds. Enamel, varnish, or charr all woodwork thoroughly, leaving no speck of wood bare and no crack open. Let the water run through and over all your ponds and apparatus for as long as possible before you begin operations.

CHAPTER VI

TROUT. MANAGEMENT OF THE OVA AND ALEVINS

Everything should now be ready for the reception of the ova. The rearing boxes are resting upon stones placed at the bottom of the ponds, with the edges some six inches above the level of the water, and moored to the sides to prevent their being moved by the current. The hatching trays are suspended in the rearing boxes, or placed upon movable rests in the boxes, with their edges just above the level of the water.

Notice is usually sent a day or two before the ova are despatched from fish cultural establishments, so the amateur has no excuse for not being absolutely ready for their reception. They are packed in various ways, and nowadays suffer but little in the transit. The ova should always be carefully washed before they are placed in the hatching trays. Mr. Armistead, in *A Handy Guide to Fish Culture*, says:--"If just turned out of a packing case there may be small pieces of moss or other material amongst them. In any case a wash will do them no harm, and the process is a very simple one. Take a pail, half-filled with ova, and then fill up with water, and with a small lading-can lift some of the water out, and pour it back again, so as to cause a downward current, which will agitate the ova. Their specific gravity being greater than that of water, they immediately retire again to the bottom of the pail, and by at once pouring off as much water as is practicable, any floating particles of moss, etc., may be carried off. Should any be left, the process should be repeated, and it may even be necessary to repeat it several times. When all is right take a ladle, or small vessel of some kind, say a good-sized tea-cup, and gently ladle out the eggs, and place them roughly on the grills, where they may be roughly spread by means of a feather."

To these instructions I would add some for the amateur, who will probably deal with a comparatively small number of ova. The ova should be washed in some large vessel full of water in the manner above described. When the water is quite clear, and the ova clean, they may be caught in mid-water as they are sinking either in the hatching trays or in a cup. If caught in a cup they should be transferred with great care to the hatching trays, and spread out in a single and somewhat spare layer. They must on no account be poured into the trays from a height. While under water well-eyed ova will stand a good deal of gentle tumbling about, but if dropped into the water from even a little height the concussion is likely to kill them.

Mr. Armistead recommends glass grills rather than trays such as I have described, but I have found the trays work very well, and they are very simple and clean. Glass grills are, however, very excellent, though they necessitate a somewhat greater initial outlay than do the perforated zinc trays.

A German fish culturist has recently recommended keeping a stock of fresh-water shrimps (*Gammarus pulex*) in the hatching trays and rearing boxes. He says that the shrimps eat only the dead ova, and never touch the living ones. They also eat any vegetable or animal *débris*. I have never tried the experiment myself, and so cannot speak from experience.

Dead ova should be always removed at once, and the hatching trays should be gone over carefully once or twice a day to see if any are present in them. Dead ova are easily recognized from the fact that they become opaque and white. They are best removed with a glass tube. The thumb is placed over one end of the tube, and the other end brought directly over the dead ovum. When the thumb is removed from the end of the tube held in the hand the water will rush up into the tube, carrying with it the dead ovum. The thumb is then replaced over the end of the tube, which is lifted from the water with the ovum retained in it. This tube may also be used for removing any extraneous bodies which may get into the trays or boxes.

A form of fungus known as *Byssus* grows upon dead ova, and it is principally for this reason that they must be removed. Livingstone Stone says of *Byssus*:--"With trout eggs in water at 40° or 50° Fahrenheit, it generally appears within forty-eight hours after the egg turns white, and often sooner, and the warmer the water the quicker it comes. It is never quite safe to leave the dead eggs over twenty-four hours in the hatching boxes. The peculiarity of *Byssus* is that it stretches out its long, slender arms, which grow rapidly over everything within its reach. This makes it peculiarly mischievous, for it will sometimes clasp a dozen or even twenty eggs in its Briarean grasp before it is discovered, and any egg that it has seized has received its death warrant." Mr. Armistead has known it appear within twenty-four hours. *Byssus* develops only on dead ova.

Saprolegnia, known to fish culturists as "fungus," attacks both living or dead ova. If the woodwork is properly varnished or charred, and the ova managed thoroughly, there should, however, be but little risk of fungus. Light is favourable to the growth of fungus, and, therefore, wooden lids should be placed over the rearing boxes. These should be kept partially on after the young fish have hatched out, and be replaced by covers of fine wire netting spread on closely-fitting frames, when the fry have begun to feed. These obviate the necessity of covering up the ponds during the first stages.

Many small creatures such as caddis-worms will eat the ova, and therefore a careful watch should be kept upon the hatching trays as it is marvellous how such creatures find their way in, in spite of all precautions. Birds of several kinds are also likely to cause great damage unless the ova and young fish are carefully guarded from their depredations.

In a short time, probably within a few days of receiving the ova, the amateur will find that the young fish are beginning to hatch out. They generally come out tail first, and in wriggling this about in their attempts to get further out, they propel the ovum about the bottom of the tray. When the little fish attempts to come out head first, he sometimes gets into difficulties and if this is observed, he may be helped by a gentle touch with a feather or a camel's hair brush.

When first hatched out the young fish have a large translucent protuberance on the under-surface. This is the umbilical or yolk-sac, and contains the nourishment upon which the little fish lives during the first stage of its life after it is hatched. This sac is gradually absorbed but until it is absorbed the young fish are called "alevins." At first the little fish do not require any food, but they generally begin to feed in about six weeks, and before the yolk-sac is completely absorbed. The rearing boxes should be kept partly covered, and the alevins will crowd into a pack in the darker parts at the bottom of the hatching tray.

The shells of the ova must be removed from the hatching trays. As they are lighter than the alevins, the current will generally carry them to the lower end of the tray, whence they may be removed with a piece of gauze spread on a wire ring, or by raising and lowering the tray gently in the water in alternately slanting directions.

The alevin stage is the stage in which the least mortality should be expected, and the little fish give but little trouble. There are, however, several diseases besides fungus (of which I have spoken already when dealing with the ova) from which the alevins may suffer.

I was, I believe, the first to describe (in the "Rainbow Trout") a peculiar disease from which alevins suffered. When hatched out and kept in water containing a very large quantity of air in solution, I found that sometimes alevins developed an air bubble in the yolk-sac. On developing this bubble they are unable to stay at the bottom as they usually do, but swim about on their backs at the surface, with part of the yolk-sac out of the water. An effectual cure for this is to put the affected alevins into still water for about thirty-six hours. I have observed this affection in the alevins of the rainbow trout (*Salmo irideus*), the common trout (*S. fario*) and the Quinnat or Californian Salmon (*Onchorynchus conicha*).

"Blue Swelling" of the yolk-sac is another disease from which alevins sometimes suffer, but I have never heard of any cure for this. Another, "paralysis," may be caused by lack of sufficient current and by insufficient aeration of the water. Sickly alevins will, as a rule, drop out of the pack, and lie on the bottom or against the end of the hatching tray, where they are carried by the current.

Dead alevins should be removed at once, and for this reason it is necessary that the hatching trays should be examined at least once a day.

CHAPTER VII

TROUT. MANAGEMENT OF THE FRY

A greatly varying period of time having elapsed and the yolk-sacs of the alevins being nearly absorbed, the fish culturist will see that some of the little fish begin to leave the pack at the bottom of the tray, and to swim up against the current. When this is observed some very finely divided food should be offered to these alevins. They will probably dart at the minute pieces of food floating past and a little more may then be given to them. If, however, they do not take any notice of little pieces of food or any other matter which floats past them, they should not be tried again till the next day. In a few days from the first of the alevins beginning to feed, all of them will be working up with their heads to the current, darting at any particles floating in the water. The tray should now be lowered so that its edge is some three or four inches below the surface and the little fish allowed to swim out into the box.

As soon as the yolk-sacs of the alevins are absorbed the little fish cease to be alevins, and are called "fry."

The alevin stage was that in which the fish give least trouble, the stage I am now describing is that in which they give most. They must be fed frequently--at least four times a day. "Little and often" is the maxim which should rule the actions of the fish culturist with regard to feeding the fry. If he can only feed his fish four times a day, he must spend some time on each of these four occasions. The food must not be thrown in all at once. If this be done the little fish will not get half of it; the other half will sink to the bottom.

The food should be introduced in small quantities at a time, and if the amateur has several boxes he should put a little food into each in succession, coming back to the first when he has put some into the last, repeating this operation at least half a dozen times. The less he puts in at each time, and the oftener he does it, the better. The ideal plan would be to put a very small quantity of food in each time, and to go on doing this at intervals of from five to ten minutes all day.

Livingstone Stone says, "You need not be afraid of the young fry's eating too much." And again, "I never knew any healthy young fry of mine decline eating but once, and then I had fed them incessantly for two hours, at the end of which time they gave up, beaten." Personally, I have found no limit to the time that the fry will continue feeding. I have kept on putting small quantities of food into a rearing box for a whole afternoon, and I was tired of feeding before the fry were tired of eating. My reader will infer from this that I believe that the fry cannot be over-fed, and this is to a certain extent true. If finely divided food is given in such small quantities that practically none of it sinks to the bottom without their having a fair chance at it, I believe that in a box containing only a couple of thousand fry, it would be found that they never stopped feeding during the whole day. If, however, too large pieces of food are offered to the little fish, many of them are likely to be choked and to die, from trying to swallow a piece a little too big for them.

The amateur will observe that shortly after the fry have been let out into the box and are feeding freely, they will separate into two more or less distinct groups. One at the upper end where the current comes in and is strongest, and one at the lower end. The fish at the upper end are the strongest and largest. This difference becomes more marked as time goes on, and in six or eight weeks after they have begun to feed the larger fish will be almost double the size of the smaller. In the middle of April, if many fry are in each box, they should be thinned out, and other boxes brought into use. The smaller fish may then be taken from one or two boxes and put into another by themselves. In feeding care should be taken that the small and weakly fish get a fair share of the food.

No matter how carefully the feeding is managed, some of the food is sure to escape the young fish and sink to the bottom. This, if left as it is, will decay and cause great mischief. A very simple and easily applied remedy for this evil exists in the use of mould dissolved in the water. Livingstone Stone recommends the mould under a sod, and I have always used this with the most beneficial effect. Earth, besides covering up and deodorizing the decomposing food at the bottom, also contains some materials which are apparently necessary to the well-being of trout. To quote again from Livingstone Stone, who was the discoverer of this use of mould: "Earth or mud is the last thing one would suppose suitable for a fish so associated in our minds with pure, clean water; yet it is an indispensable constituent in the diet of young trout, and unless they get it, either naturally or artificially, they will not thrive."

The effect of earth given in this way upon the young fish is simply marvellous. They become more lively and feed more freely. This is the effect of a spate--which is, after all, only a dose of earth--upon wild trout.

The mould should be mixed with water in a bucket, and, when the water is very thick and muddy, poured into the rearing boxes. The water in the rearing boxes should be so thick that neither the bottom nor the young fish, except when they come to the surface to take some passing particle of food, can be seen. The amateur should not wait till something goes wrong before giving this dose of earth; it is advisable to give it once a week at any rate, and oftener if the fish seem to be ailing in any way.

In dealing with the subject of food for the young fish, I would begin by impressing upon my reader that the greater variety of food he can give the better it will be for the fish. He should also give them, at any rate after they have been feeding some weeks, a certain proportion of natural food. Probably the best of all food for the fry is pounded shrimps or other crustaceans. It is, however, difficult in the very early stages of the trout's life to pound shrimps up small enough, and the little fish are much given to trying to swallow pieces of food which are too large for them to manage. This evil proclivity often causes the death of the fry, and therefore great care must be taken that no pieces of food which are too large, get into the rearing box. Pounded liver shaken up in a bottle with water, and after the larger particles have been allowed to settle at the bottom, poured into the rearing box in small quantities, is a good form of food for the alevins when they first begin to feed. The yolks of eggs boiled for about half an hour and pounded up, dog biscuit very finely pounded, or the fine food supplied by several of the fish cultural establishments are also excellent. In giving moist food such as pounded shrimps, liver, meat, or the yolks of eggs, a good plan while the fry are very small is to put the food in a small net made of fine muslin mounted on a wire ring, and dipping the end of this net into the water, allow small particles to escape through the muslin. This ensures no large pieces getting into the rearing boxes. As the fry grow larger, these precautions are of course modified, as the little fish are capable of swallowing larger pieces of food.

With regard to natural food, the amateur should take care to ensure a good stock for the young fish. Many of the creatures suitable for food may be cultivated in separate ponds at the same time as the fish, if a natural supply is not at hand. The *Daphnia pulex* (water flea) and the *Cyclops quadricornis* may be introduced into the boxes very soon after the fish have began to feed. *Daphnia* breeds at the rate which is almost inconceivable. The female produces her first brood of young when she is ten days old, and goes on breeding at an average of three or four times a month. The female and her progeny are rendered fertile by one act of coition, probably for fifteen generations at least, without any further intervention of the male. Both *Daphnia* and

Cyclops are bred in stagnant water in which there should be a good stock of weeds.

The fresh water shrimp (*Gammarus pulex*) is an excellent form of food for young and old trout, and should be given to the fry as soon as they are old enough to manage them. *Corixæ* and other small insects should also be given as often as possible. The fresh-water shrimp is bred in running water, *Corixæ* in still or slow running water. Weeds are necessary to the well-being of both.

The boxes must be kept carefully covered, as I have already pointed out. A kingfisher would make short work of a box of fry, and other birds and beasts of various kinds are partial to them. There are only two courses open to the fish culturist in dealing with these enemies--to protect his fish or kill the enemies. I prefer to protect the fish first and kill the enemies afterwards.

The greatest care must be taken not to introduce, or allow to intrude, any water beetles or the larger carnivorous aquatic larvæ of insects, into the rearing boxes. I have known cases where the larvæ of the *Dytiscus marginalis*, the largest of our carnivorous water beetles, have destroyed almost all the fry in a rearing pond. The adult *D. marginalis* itself is not a whit less voracious, and much stronger than its larva.

If the wooden parts of the apparatus have been properly prepared, according to my previous instructions, there should be no risk of the fry developing fungus. Quite a small spot of woodwork, however, left uncovered by asphalt-varnish, or enamel, or uncharred, will render the chance of the development of this disease probable.

Should by any misfortune fungus get into the rearing boxes, a dose of salt may very likely cure it. Sea water is the best, but if this is not obtainable, a solution of salt and water run through the boxes will probably cure the disease. Considerable good may also be done to the young fish by occasionally putting a lump of rock salt in at the inlet, and the water allowed to run over and dissolve it.

CHAPTER VIII

TROUT. THE MANAGEMENT OF THE FRY (*Continued*)

In the last chapter I brought my reader up to the point where the fry, which had been feeding for some time in the rearing boxes, had been judiciously separated, the weaker and smaller fish which took up their positions at the lower ends of the boxes having been put into separate boxes and induced as much as possible to keep at the head near to where the current enters.

It is difficult to lay down any certain rule as to what is the best time at which to take the next step--that of turning the fry out into the rearing ponds. When the fry have got into more or less regular habits, and showing no fear of whoever it is who feeds them, come up readily and seize the food boldly, is probably the best time to let them out into the larger space of the pond. I do not mean to say that when a certain proportion of the fish have got over their natural shyness, and feed boldly and without hesitation, the whole of them should be set free. What I mean is, that when the habit of associating the appearance of a certain individual with a meal has been well established among them for a week or so, they should be allowed to escape from the box into the pond.

This is best done in the same way that the alevins were allowed to escape from the hatching tray into the box--by lowering the level of the box so that its upper edges are some two or three inches below the surface of the water. The food should now be thrown into the pond higher up, so that the little fish may be induced to swim up and station themselves as near the inlet as possible. Probably some of the little fish will not leave the box at all of their own free will. These, of course, will have to be turned out. The box should not, however, be lifted out of the water and the fish and water together be poured out, as this is very likely to cause them severe injury. The box should be gradually tilted over and lifted out of the water bottom first, so that the fish are hardly disturbed at all and certainly not injured in any way.

An important matter to consider before turning the little fish out into the pond is, how the ponds are to be protected so that their many enemies may be kept away from the fry. Kingfishers, herons, and other creatures are very partial to young trout and will cause enormous destruction if not prevented. Kingfishers have, in my experience, been the worst offenders. Some years ago I was rearing some trout in a part of the country where many of the inhabitants bewailed the extermination of the kingfisher. Before I began rearing trout I agreed with these people, for a kingfisher flitting along a stream looking like a little mass of jewels is a pleasing sight, and one which I had never enjoyed in that particular part of the country.

When the time came to set my little fish free in the rearing ponds, as a matter of principle I covered the ponds with herring-net, closely pegged down on the banks so that I could not even get my hand under the edge. I did not think that there were any kingfishers or herons about, and so was very surprised when one morning, on going down to feed the fish, I found a kingfisher under the net, flying up and down the pond trying to get out. By carefully introducing a landing-net under the netting over the pond, I was able to catch the intruder, and caught four more in the same way in about three weeks. Since that time I have not agreed with the people who have stated that the kingfisher is almost extinct, at least in that part of the country. I may say that there are but few streams there, and that it is not at all an apparently likely place for kingfishers. I am quite sure that wherever any one begins to rear fish there he will find that kingfishers are fairly common. The amateur will probably be also surprised at the way herons appear, if he conducts his fish-rearing operations, as he should do, in a secluded spot.

Many of the directions I gave as to the management of the fry and the rearing boxes, apply also to the fry after they have been turned out into the ponds. The doses of earth should still be given regularly, and salt may be applied also in the way I have already described. The little fish will be found to scatter over the pond or to divide again into two bodies, one at the upper and one at the lower end of the pond, as they did in the boxes. The fish culturist should try to induce these fish to come to the head of the pond as much as possible. It is a good thing to place some boards across the head of the pond to give shade and shelter to the fry. It will probably be found that if much artificial food is given to the little fish, a scum will be formed on the surface of the water. This scum is composed of grease, and should be removed, as soon as it is observed, with a gauze net.

All the time that these operations have been going on with regard to the little fish themselves, due attention should have been given to the vegetation round the ponds. The alders and willows which I before recommended to be planted round the ponds should be induced as much as possible to overhang the water. Grass and other vegetation should be allowed to grow freely round the margins, as many insects are then likely to fall into the water.

This vegetation will supply the little fish with a certain amount of natural floating food, without any interference on the part of the fish culturist; but he should, however, give them other floating food, both natural and artificial, as much as possible, for this will get them in their youth to adopt the habit of feeding freely at the surface. When the alders and willows have grown sufficiently and are well covered with leaves, they will probably give enough shelter to the fish to make the boards at the upper end of the pond unnecessary.

As time goes on, and the little fish grow, they should be thinned out, the smaller and weaker being removed into another pond.

Despite the best endeavours of the fish culturist, a certain number of these small fish are sure to keep to the lower end of the pond, and it is these which should be removed first. If they are left, the difference in size between the smaller and the larger will soon become so great that the large fish will very likely be tempted to eat the small ones, thus developing a cannibalistic habit which they will keep always.

At the end of August or the beginning of September the little fish will have got over the most dangerous part of their lives. After this time they are called yearlings, are much more hardy and not subject to nearly as many risks as up to that time.

The great points to remember are:--That the food should be varied as much as possible; and as much natural food, of a hard description such as shrimps, *corixæ*, snails, bivalves, etc., be given. That the little fish should be well protected from enemies. That they should not be over-crowded, but the weakly and small fish be separated from the larger fish. That frequent doses of earth should be given to keep the bottom sweet and clean.[2] That the inlets and outlets should be frequently cleaned and kept clear, to ensure a good flow of water through the ponds, and that a careful watch should be kept for such misfortunes as fungus and dead fish, in order that they may be dealt with at once.

[2] See two letters in Appendix.--Page 93

CHAPTER IX

TROUT. THE FRIENDS AND ENEMIES OF THE FISH
CULTURIST

The creatures which are sometimes found in and around rearing
ponds containing ova or young fish are very numerous, and it is
advisable that the fish culturist should have some knowledge of
them. It is for this reason, that while I cautioned my readers
against the creatures which are dangerous, and enumerated
some of those most serviceable as food, I left detailed
descriptions of these enemies and friends of the little fish, in
order that I might deal with them in a separate chapter.

[Illustration: LARVA OF *DYTISCUS* AND YOUNG TROUT.]

Among the worst enemies of both ova and fry is the *Dytiscus
marginalis*, whether this insect be in the larval or adult stage. I
think that I should hardly be wrong in going even further and
saying that *D. marginalis* is very dangerous to trout early in their
yearling stage. The accompanying illustration shows a larva of
Dytiscus which has caught a young trout. This illustration is
taken from a photograph of a specimen lent to me by Mr. F. M.
Halford, and both the fish and the larva were alive when they
were caught. Unfortunately the trout is a little shrivelled, and the
legs of the *Dytiscus* have been broken. *D. marginalis* lays its
eggs in the stems of rushes. The larva, when hatched, makes its
way out, and proceeds to lead a predatory life. The larva when
full-grown is about two inches long, and is quite the most
rapacious creature which lives in our waters. The adult beetle is
also purely carnivorous, but is perhaps not quite so rapacious. It
would, however, probably attack a larger fish.

The largest of English water beetles is *Hydrophilus piceus*. This
beetle is not, in the adult stage at least, carnivorous, but the
larva, which is about half an inch longer and considerably fatter

than that of *D. marginalis*, is carnivorous. It may be told from the larva of *Dytiscus* not only by its size, which is hardly a reliable point for discrimination, but by the smaller size of the head in comparison to the rest of the body. The claws, with which *Hydrophilus* seizes its prey, are, too, considerably smaller than those of *Dytiscus*. This larva should be kept out of the rearing ponds with just as much care as that of the more voracious *D. marginalis*.

With the kingfisher I have already dealt at some length, so that I need say but little more with regard to it. One of the worst features in this bird's character is that it will go on killing many more little fish than it can possibly eat. As I have before said, it is surprising how these birds will appear in considerable numbers where a fish hatchery is started, even in localities where they have before been considered rare. I have already described how the ponds should be protected from their ravages.

Herons do a great deal of harm to fish ponds, even when the fish have got well into the yearling stage. I have on one or two occasions known of herons wounding trout of at least a pound in weight. Besides the actual damage they do by killing fish, they put all the other fish in the pond off their feed through frightening them. After a heron or kingfisher has been about a rearing pond the little fish will not feed for a considerable time, sometimes even for days. Notwithstanding their very evil proclivities, both herons and kingfishers are very interesting. A kingfisher, if he catches a fish which is a little too big for him to swallow whole, will knock the head of the fish, which he always catches by the middle of the body, against a stone, in order to kill it, or at least to stop it struggling; it might otherwise in its struggles escape, as the kingfisher can only swallow a fish head first. There are stories which tell how herons sometimes pluck small feathers from their breasts and, floating these feathers upon the water, catch the trout as they rise to it; it is supposed that the trout takes the feather for a fly. Personally, I do not think that much credence should be attached to the latter story.

Other birds, usually found on or near the water, are also likely to do much harm to the ova and young fish. Almost every creature which is found near the water seems to have a great liking for the ova of fishes. All the wading and swimming birds are to be dreaded by the fish culturist. They will, all of them, eat ova in enormous quantities, and many of them will also eat the little fish.

Besides birds, small larvæ of several insects will eat, or at any rate kill, the ova in considerable numbers. Caddis-worms are among these larvæ which eat ova. This seems to be one of the few cases in which nature is just, for caddis-worms are taken very readily by even small trout. Large trout will take them very greedily, cases and all. Therefore, I should advise the fish culturist to cultivate them as food for the fish he is rearing, but to be very careful that they do not get into the rearing boxes or hatching trays when he has ova in them. The caddis-worms kill the ova by making a small hole in them and sucking some of the contents out; from this hole some more of the contents escapes, and as it comes into contact with the water becomes opaque.

Caddis-worms are the larvæ of an order of four-winged flies commonly known as sedges, caddis-flies, or water-moths. The latter appellation is of course a misnomer, as these flies (*Trichoptera*) have nothing whatever to do with moths. They resemble moths, however, in that they have four wings which when at rest lie in much the same position as do those of moths, and as many of them have their wings thickly covered with hairs, this resemblance is sometimes very marked. The larvæ (caddis-worms), being eagerly sought as food by many fish, and having very soft bodies, make for themselves cases. Some of these cases are made from small sticks, some from little pieces of stone or sand, and some from a mixture of all of these substances. As these cases resemble such small pieces of rubbish as are frequently found in streams, care should be taken that they do not get into the hatching trays containing ova.

Many of the water beetles, and practically all of their larvæ, will attack the ova; they should therefore be carefully excluded from the hatching trays. As there are about 114 different species of beetles in the family of *Dytiscidæ* alone, my readers will appreciate my reason for not attempting to enumerate them. It will be a sufficient warning to state the fact that they are all carnivorous, and their relative sizes is the only thing which will decide whether the beetle will eat the fish, or the fish the beetle.

Very similar to beetles are some of the water-bugs. They may, however, easily be distinguished from beetles, as the outer or anterior wings of the bugs cross each other at their lower ends, while the elytra of beetles, which much resemble the horny, anterior wings of some of the water-bugs, meet exactly in the middle line. These water-bugs, though some of them are excellent food for even the small fish, will attack the ova, and therefore they should be kept out of the hatching trays. The fish culturist should, however, whenever it is possible, cultivate such of these water-bugs as are good food for the fry in separate ponds, as I have before recommended. The best of these water-bugs are *Corixæ*. Others, such as the water-boatman, water-scorpions and pond-skaters, are not of any value as food for the fish.

The larvæ of *Ephemeridæ* are very good food for the fish, and should be cultivated in separate ponds if possible, and some turned into the ponds containing the little fish occasionally. A fair proportion should, however, be kept in the ponds and protected, so that a good stock of the flies may be available next year.

The larvæ of *Ephemeridæ* may be obtained in many streams, and are best caught with a fine gauze net. Some of them swim, but most are generally captured with such a net at the bottom of

the water among the *débris*. Eggs of *Ephemeridæ* may be
obtained sometimes from another locality if they cannot be got
on the spot. These should be carefully preserved for the first
year at any rate, and a good fly may thus be introduced into a
water where it was before unknown.

I have already spoken of the fresh-water shrimp and the
water-flea (*Daphnia pulex*). These valuable articles of diet should
be introduced whenever it is possible. *Daphnia* must be reared in
a stagnant pond, the fresh-water shrimp (*Gammarus pulex*) in
running water, with plenty of weeds.

Other useful creatures besides those snails and mussels which I
described in a previous chapter, are the water-louse (*Asellus
aquaticus*), *Cypridæ*, and *Cyclops quadricornis*. Asellus is very
similar in size and shape to the common garden-louse, which is
found in decaying wood. It will live either in stagnant or running
water. *Cypridæ* are very much smaller, being generally only as
large as a large pin's head. They have a bivalve shell which
makes them look something like a small mussel. They are,
however, very active, swimming by means of two pairs of legs.
They also possess two pairs of antennæ and one eye. (The
species belonging to the genus *Candona* of the family *Cypridæ*,
do not swim.) *Cyclops* is another very small crustacean, shaped
like a large-headed club. It swims very actively, and, like the
Cypridæ, is an excellent article of diet for very young fish. Both
these crustacea live in stagnant water, and must, therefore, be
kept in a separate pond, whence they may be taken as required
to be given to the fry.

CHAPTER X

TROUT. MANAGEMENT, FEEDING, AND TURNING OUT OF
YEARLINGS

As I pointed out to my readers in Chapter VIII., the young trout
have after August passed the critical period of their existence,
and may be considered safe and hardy. Naturally, as they get
older, they require more food, but this need not be given so
frequently as the fish grow older. While it was necessary to feed
the fry at least four times a day, it will be found quite sufficient if
the fish in August are fed only twice during the twenty-four hours.
I must here again impress upon my reader the importance of
feeding the trout upon as natural a food as possible. Their future
well-being depends upon this, much more than is generally
realized even by fish culturists. Of course, trout fed entirely upon
soft food may turn out all right, particularly if they are turned out
as very young yearlings, but it is better not to leave anything to
chance and make sure of being on the safe side.

As was the case with the fry during the whole of the earlier part
of their lives, the yearlings will divide into two more or less
separate packs, though the fish may have been separated
several times before in order to divide those which kept at the
head from those which kept at the lower end of the pond. Those
trout at the lower end must be coaxed to the upper end as much
as possible, care being taken when feeding that all the fish get a
fair share of food. Should any of the fish remain obstinately at
the lower end, and those at the upper end outgrow them to a
marked extent, the smaller ones must be again separated from
the larger.

When, in September or October, the little fish have grown active
and strong, they may be turned out into the water they are to
occupy for the rest of their lives. There is really no reason why, if
they are well-grown and strong, they should not be turned out in

August if the water they have to be taken to is quite close to the rearing ponds, but if they have to be carried any distance, it is better to keep them in the rearing ponds for a few weeks longer, till the weather gets cool enough to make it quite safe to allow for a possible delay in the transit.

The turning out of the fish requires some little care. I have seen fish which had been sent by rail, poured out with the water contained in the cans, in as hurried a manner as possible. Though of course it is important to get the fish out of the cans used for transport as soon as is compatible with safety; still, undue haste in this operation is likely to do much harm. Young fish of any kind require delicate handling, and young trout particularly. The cans should, when possible, be partly emptied, and some water from that into which they are to be turned put into the can. This is of course not necessary if the rearing ponds are supplied from the same source as the water into which the fish are turned. The cans should then be partially immersed in the water, and the edges brought gradually below the surface. This allows the fish to swim out of the cans of their own accord, and the few which will not go out may be forced to do so by gently turning the can upside down.

It is a very good thing to give each of the fish a dose of salt before turning them out, particularly if they have travelled any distance. This is easily managed by catching the fish, a few at a time, in a landing-net from the travelling can, and then, instead of putting them straight into the water, putting them into a bucket of salt and water for a short time. Sea water is of course better if it is available. This does away with any risk of their developing fungus on the spots which have very likely got bruised during the journey.

The yearlings are best taken from the rearing ponds by netting them. A net which is more than broad enough to go across the rearing pond is necessary. Too many should not be taken out at a time in each haul of the net, as they are thus more likely to be injured or dropped on the ground. The amateur should not forget, that though the little fish will stand a good deal of moving about as long as they are in water, they are likely to be killed, or at least severely injured, by a shock, particularly if that shock is sustained while they are out of the water for a second or two during their being moved from one place to another.

If the amateur intends to keep any of his yearlings longer than December, he will have to make a larger pond. This pond need not be a long, narrow one like those in which the fry were kept. Though the fish of course still require a sufficient supply of well-aerated water, a larger pond without the same marked current through it will do perfectly well. They must be well fed, and if any grow markedly bigger than the rest these should be separated. If they are not well supplied with food they are very likely to try and eat each other, that is to say, the largest will try to eat the smallest.

CHAPTER XI

THE REARING OF THE RAINBOW TROUT, AMERICAN BROOK TROUT, AND CHAR

As the methods used in hatching out the ova and rearing the young fish are very similar in the case of different species of trout to those I have already described in dealing with the common trout (*Salmo fario*), I will confine myself to pointing out the most marked differences in the habits of such species as are suitable to our waters, and which are likely to be of use to the fish culturist. The salmon- or sea-trout will be dealt with under salmon.

First and foremost among the trout, excluding of course our own brown trout, I put the rainbow trout (*Salmo irideus*). There are several varieties of this species, but that which is now being so freely introduced into many waters in England is the McCloud River rainbow (*S. irideus*, var. *shasta*). As I have before stated, the rainbow spawns long after the *S. fario*. It therefore will give the fly-fishermen good sport after the season for the common trout is over. It is a very free feeder, and grows more rapidly than our trout; great care must therefore be taken to give it plenty of food. I would draw my readers' attention particularly to this fact as to the feeding and quick-growing qualities of the rainbow, for they make it, if possible, even more necessary that the water into which they are turned should contain a good supply of food than it was in the case of the common trout; though even in the case of the common trout, this is quite the most important consideration in stocking a water with fish.

Another advantage possessed by the rainbow is, that it is less liable to the attacks of fungus than any other of the *Salmonidæ*. Though, of course, this is not such an important consideration nowadays as it would have been even a few years ago, still it is one which deserves some consideration, particularly from the amateur. This freedom from fungus is very marked in the rainbow, for I know of a case where some dace suffering from fungus were put into a rearing pond containing a few rainbows. Though the dace died of the disease, the rainbows remained healthy and free from it. The amateur will probably receive the ova of the rainbow towards the end of April or during May. The ova should hatch out within a few days of their being received.

A few years, I might almost say months ago, the great majority of disinterested persons, whose opinion was of any consequence, were inclined to condemn the general introduction of this fish into our waters. I was, unfortunately, supposed to be among a certain class of people who advocated the general introduction of this fish into all our waters indiscriminately. This, I have always said, was a very short-sighted policy, for, to begin with, the evidence at our disposal seems to show that the rainbow will never thrive in cold waters, and at the best can only be expected to really thrive and spawn in the warm waters in the south of England. I never advocated more for the rainbow than that it should have a fair trial in waters where our own trout had been tried and found not to be a success. Now, however, I in my turn stand a chance of being converted by converts from among the very people who, a short time ago, were condemning me for holding too favourable an opinion of the fish in question. I am inclined to think that in the case of a pond in the south, even when it is supplied by a good stream, the rainbow is the better fish with which to stock. I have been led to believe this, partly through my own experience, and partly on account of the opinion of Mr. Senior, for I consider his opinion on such a matter of the greatest possible value.

Another point about the rainbow, which in many cases will recommend it particularly to the amateur, is that though of course an abundant supply of water is an advantage, it may be reared with a smaller supply.

A fish which has been very freely introduced into British waters is the American brook-trout (*Salvelinus fontinalis*). Though this fish is not really a trout but a char I have included it among trout, because it is so very generally known to fishermen as the American brook-trout. The *fontinalis*, as it is commonly called by fish culturists, is a very satisfactory fish to rear artificially, but there seems to be some doubt as to its suitability to British waters. It grows to a considerable size under favourable conditions, and is one of the best of table fishes. It is, however, undoubtedly one of the worst of cannibals among sporting fishes, and does not apparently rise freely to the fly when about two years old and older.

The spawning season is extended over an even longer period than that of our own brown trout, beginning, in its native country, in October, and sometimes lasting till March. It shows a very marked tendency, at any rate in America, to go down to the sea, and in some parts of Canada is called a sea-trout. The fish are easy to rear, but I should recommend great caution with regard to their introduction into any waters in England. The remarks and instructions which I gave with regard to the common trout, apply also to the *fontinalis*, but I would lay particular stress upon the necessity of separating the fish, as soon as some grow larger than the rest. The only drawback to this fish, from the fish culturist's point of view, is that though a very free feeder, it is very dainty, sometimes refusing a particular kind of food for no apparent reason. As the spawning season is extended over such a considerable period of time, it is obvious that the amateur will be able to obtain the ova, ready to hatch out, during a similarly lengthy period.

A fish which I should very much like to see tried in England, is the cut-throat trout (*Salmo mykiss*). It is also known as the red-throat trout. I should think, from the description given in the report of the Commission of Fisheries, Game, and Forests for the State of New York, that it would do well in many of our waters. There are many varieties of this species of trout. The common name of them all is *Salmo mykiss*, the black-spotted trout of the Rocky Mountains. The cut-throat trout proper, so called from the red colour of its throat, is simply S. mykiss, but there are many varieties described. Among these are the Columbia River trout (*S. mykiss*, var. *clarkii*), the Lake Tahoe trout (*S. mykiss*, var. *henshawi*), the Rio Grande trout (*S. mykiss*, var. *spilurus*), and the Colorado River trout (*S. mykiss*, var. *pleuriticus*). As these names show, the black-spotted trout has a very wide range and is found in what are totally different climates. I should very much like to see the cut-throat and the Columbia River varieties tried in our waters, particularly the former, as they would probably succeed in waters which are too cold for the rainbow, and might very likely thrive where our own trout (*S. fario*) is not a success. As it is found in climates which vary so much as do Alaska and California, it would probably be easy to find one variety, if not two or three, which would thrive in England. It is a particularly fine trout, and the ordinary maximum weight is five or six pounds, though some of the varieties grow much larger.

Char, proper, are not at all satisfactory fish to rear. They are very delicate, and require much more care and attention than do any of the fish I have already described. From the very first period of their coming under the care of the amateur fish culturist, that is to say, from the ova, just before hatching out, till they are yearlings, the mortality among them will be much greater than in the case of any of the trout.

The two kinds of char, most commonly to be obtained by the amateur, are the Alpine and the Windermere char. The ova of these fish will be received shortly before they are ready to hatch out, as was the case with the trout ova. The amateur's difficulties will, however, begin almost at once, for in the act of hatching out considerable mortality among the char often occurs. Trout almost invariably emerge from the egg tail first. As soon as the tail is free the little fish begins to move it rapidly, using it as a propeller with which to swim about and thus soon works completely out of the egg. Occasionally, however, trout hatch out head first, and in these cases the young fish generally dies before it can set itself free from the coverings of the ovum. Buckland observed that the alevins of the char very frequently hatch out head first, and consequently that many of them die before they can work themselves free from the eggs. If it were possible to have some one constantly watching the ova at the time that they are hatching out, it would be possible to save a very large proportion of them, as they may be very effectually helped out of the egg with a feather or soft camel's-hair brush; but this is, of course, quite impracticable, unless there is some one constantly watching the ova, as the delay of even a few minutes will mean the death of the fish. This peculiarity in the hatching out of the char has also been observed by Mr. J. J. Armistead, and I have been able to verify it personally.

The mortality which occurs in the actual hatching out of the alevins does not, however, by any means end the trouble which the fish culturist has to encounter in the rearing of char. They require much more persuasion and care when they begin to feed and throughout the whole of the summer. The percentage of deaths is always greater than in the case of the trouts, not excluding the *fontinalis*, which is, as I have already explained, not really a trout but a char.

Though there must be some doubt as to its success, I should like to see a really serious attempt at introducing char into some deep and large ponds in the south of England. Char have been very successfully reared in shallow water, which was certainly not kept at a particularly low temperature, so I see no reason why this fish should not do in some of our more southern waters. One drawback to the chance of this attempt being made, however, is that the char cannot be considered as being a fish which gives very good sport, and I very much doubt whether any one is likely to try the experiment simply to find out whether they would or would not succeed in the south of England.

CHAPTER XII

SALMON AND SEA-TROUT

In many ways nature is apparently very wasteful, and in nothing is this more marked than in the case of the salmon. Probably not more than one egg in a thousand produces a fish which reaches the smolt stage, and a still smaller proportion grows to the spawning stage. This great mortality which occurs among the eggs and young fish when left to nature may be very considerably reduced by artificial means, so that a very fair proportion of the eggs deposited by the female fish will not only be hatched out successfully, but the little fish will reach the smolt stage safely and have a good chance of reaching the sea. How successful artificial intervention may be has been proved over and over again in the United States and in Canada. In the case of more than one river in Canada, the artificial propagation and protection of salmon has resulted in what is apparently the actual manufacture of a salmon river, yielding an annual haul of fish far beyond anything known in Europe, from a river which before yielded no salmon, or hardly any.

These operations, carried out by the State, were of course far beyond anything which could be undertaken by the amateur, but I am sure that if several riparian owners on a salmon river carried on artificial hatching and rearing operations for several seasons, a marked increase in the number of fish in the river would ensue. The objection of most people to this course is that it is unfortunately only too apparent that they are benefiting chiefly, not the rod fisherman, but the netsman at the mouth of the river.

The different artificial means used to help nature in producing a good head of salmon in a river vary chiefly in the amount of the help given by each. It will suffice to say that the best is that which provides for the protection and feeding of the young fish till it is ready to take its first journey to the sea. The reason of this is obvious, as every day passed in safety is a day gained, both in strength and in power of self-preservation.

Though it is possible to purchase a certain number of salmon ova, this is not at all a satisfactory way of obtaining them. To begin with, it is impossible to get them in sufficient numbers to carry out operations on a large enough scale. Salmon ova are also expensive; and it is no use working with less than half a million in several stations if the river is of any size. It is advisable that the ova should be obtained from the fish. This may be done either by collecting the ova deposited by the fish in the spawning beds or from the gravid females. The latter course necessitates the ripe female and male fish being caught and artificially spawned. As in nature, at best but a comparatively small percentage of the ova are impregnated, and by artificial spawning over ninety per cent. of them may be successfully hatched out, there can be but little doubt as to which is the better way. It is difficult to make sure of catching the fish just at the time they are ripe, so it is advisable to impound them in a fenced-off portion of the river, where they may be got at easily.

In the ripe female the ova flow out very readily, and but little pressure is necessary. Hard pressure on the abdomen should never be applied, as it is sure to injure the fish. A ripe female having been obtained, from which the ova flow readily, the female is held over a perfectly clean tin or earthenware dish--wet, but containing no water--and the ova are caused to flow into it by gently but firmly pressing the hand on the abdomen, and stroking it down towards the vent. Milt from a ripe male fish is then allowed to run over the ova in the dish, and is made to run well between them by tilting the dish about from side to side. The ova will now adhere together, and some water should be added. This water should be poured off and fresh added till the superfluous milt is washed away, when the ova should be left in the water till they separate, which will be in about twenty minutes or half an hour.

The fertilized ova thus obtained may either be laid down in artificially protected hatching beds, or may be transferred to a hatchery. The latter proceeding, of course, requires a hatching house specially built and arranged, and as this is outside the scope of the present work, I would refer my readers to larger works upon the subject, such as *An Angler's Paradise*, by J. J. Armistead. Of course, by using a hatchery a large number of the eggs will be saved, ninety per cent. of them should hatch out. This is, therefore, obviously the best way to proceed. A very much larger number of eggs will, however, be hatched out in properly-chosen artificial beds than would be the case if they were left to nature.

The necessary qualities of a good artificial bed are, a good supply of clean water which is not liable if there is a spate to deposit sediment on the eggs, protection from light, and protection from the many creatures which prey upon the ova. The hatching beds may be so arranged that the young fish may escape as soon as they like after hatching out, but it is best to watch and protect them for at any rate the first few weeks after they have begun to feed, and while continuing the feeding, to allow those of the fish that wish to escape.

The rearing of young salmon and sea-trout is practically the same as that of the common trout, except that they require more water. If kept in rearing ponds they grow more quickly than they do when left to find food for themselves. While young, the salmon is marked with transverse bars of a darker colour than the rest of the body. During the time it bears these marks it is known as a parr.[3] In about fifteen months it loses these marks and becomes quite silvery, being now known as a smolt. Shortly after assuming the smolt dress, the young salmon takes its departure to the sea. In some cases the young salmon do not appear to go down to the sea till over two years after being hatched out, but they should always be set at liberty in March, April, or May in the year following that in which they were hatched out, according to how far they have developed the smolt or silver appearance.

[3] All the trouts go through this stage, which is distinguished by "finger marks" upon the sides.

If spring water is obtainable, particularly if the water, as is usually the case, is of an even temperature throughout the year, the troubles of the fish culturist are considerably lessened. Without a building for the hatching troughs it is almost impossible in many places to guard against frost unless such a spring is available. Sediment may be avoided by putting frames covered with flannel at the inlets to the hatching beds, these will, if kept clean, prevent any sediment from coming into the ponds, and will allow plenty of water to flow in. If hatching trays are not used, the bottom of the artificial bed should be covered with clean gravel.

The time which elapses from the impregnation of the eggs to their hatching out varies according to the temperature of the water, a fairly average time is about ninety days. The ova should be watched during this time, and the dead ones removed. For a short time after they are impregnated they are fairly hardy, but from then till shortly before they hatch out the very slightest concussion will kill or seriously injure them.

The management of sea-trout ova is similar to that of salmon, and the ova are obtained in the same way. As in the case of the salmon it is best to rear the little fish artificially, till they are ready to go down to the sea; they will thus escape dangers likely to cause the loss of about eighty per cent. of their number.

The same methods and the same precautions as advised in the chapters on rearing trout should be adopted in the case of salmon and sea-trout as far as is possible, and if this is done a very large percentage of the ova should be successfully reared to the smolt stage.

CHAPTER XIII

COARSE FISH

Compared to what is known about the early part of the life history of the *Salmonidæ*, our knowledge of coarse fish is small. Fortunately, however, such lengthy and complicated proceedings as are necessary to obtain a good stock of trout are not necessary to obtain a good stock of coarse fish. If even a few rudd, perch, dace, pike, or carp are put into water where they have a good supply of food to begin with, and which is suitable otherwise for their well-being, the amateur's chief trouble after a few years, if the water is not heavily fished, will be to keep down the stock of coarse fish in proportion to the supply of food.

I have seen many cases where rudd, perch, dace and carp have increased to an enormous extent from a few fish introduced into the water. Some four years ago we put a few small rudd into a mill-pond at home, thinking that the fry they produced would serve admirably as food to the trout which also inhabited the pond. In about twenty months the pond was full of small rudd, and last year we netted out many hundred, as the water was terribly over-stocked with them. The same thing has happened in almost every case which has come to my knowledge; that is, of course, where the waters have been stocked with food, and suitable to the fish introduced.

The way in which dace will increase when put into a suitable water is, if possible, even more remarkable than what happens in the case of the rudd. I will quote one instance, which proves this very conclusively. A few years ago there were no dace in the Sussex Ouse. Pike fishermen, however, used to bring live dace to use as baits. Some of these escaped, or were set free by the fishermen at the end of their day's fishing, and now the Sussex Ouse contains more dace for its size than any other river I have ever seen.

While rudd thrive best in a pond or lake into which a stream flows, dace require a river or stream to do well. They will, however, thrive and increase rapidly in a river where trout are not a success. A muddy bottom with occasional quickly running shallows, seem to constitute the best kind of water for dace. The largest, and by far the best conditioned dace I have seen, have come from the tidal parts of rivers, where the water is brackish at high water. Dace from such a water have also the advantage of being very good eating, as they have, as a rule, not got the unpleasant muddy taste usual in this fish.

Perch and pike will thrive both in rivers and in ponds or lakes which have a supply of water from a stream or from springs. They both increase in numbers very rapidly, and when protected, are more likely to require thinning down every few years, than artificial assistance from the amateur.

The king-carp is the best fish for the amateur who wishes to obtain good bottom fishing from an absolutely stagnant pond. This fish is much bolder and a more free feeder than the common carp. It increases so rapidly in numbers, and is a hard fighting and lively fish.

Most of the coarse fish deposit a much larger number of eggs than do any of the *Salmonidæ*--that is to say, in proportion to their size. In stocking a water which contains no fish, the amateur may wish to hurry on the process of nature in the case of coarse fish; and, fortunately, this is fairly easily managed. In the case of perch, rudd, pike, and carp, but little change of water is required to hatch out the eggs. The eggs of these fish take but a short time to hatch; and if they are protected, and this protection is also given to the little fish for a few weeks, it will generally be found that an amply sufficient result is obtained. The eggs should be spread out carefully on wicker-work or the lids of baskets and kept in the light. A trickle of water which is sufficient to change the body of water in the pond in which the ova are put will, as a rule, be enough. The amateur must be careful that the pond in which he hatches the eggs does not contain any of the many enemies I have described in former chapters. If it is at all possible to protect the eggs and the little fish, it is best to hatch out the eggs in the pond which it is intended to stock, for it is exceedingly difficult to keep the newly-hatched fish in a rearing-pond on account of their very small size. It will be necessary to use muslin or flannel screens instead of perforated zinc. Care must be taken that there is not too great a flow of water, as this will cause the little fish to be drowned at the outlet screen.

APPENDIX

THE USE OF EARTH IN REARING PONDS

[From a correspondence upon the subject which appeared in *Land and Water*]

SIR,--In your last issue I have read with pleasure the eminently practical notes on fish culture by Mr. Charles Walker. He is perfectly right in all he says with reference to the useful and preventive results of the use of "common garden" earth, or vegetable mould in checking any fungoid development, *Saprolegnia* or other. It must, however, be admitted that the said addition is not an element of beauty in a box; therefore it should be avoided, or only used when necessity dictates. However, the fry, when thoroughly restored to health, may be transferred by muslin net to another box free from earth should it be necessary to count out certain numbers for the satisfaction of customers' orders. Again, the earth employed may, and in some waters does, give rise to other ill effects on the health of the "fry" or young fishes. Affection of the eye is not unheard of as the result of over-use of earth. Perhaps the best way to obviate any trouble of this nature would be to pound and dry the earth, and keep it in a canister or other closed vessel till required for use. Spores of fungi are nearly, if not quite, omnipresent; and their effects are so insidious that too many precautions cannot well be taken to avert the introduction of "trouble" in the hatchery. Indeed, were it not for the risks arising from attacks of fungi, pisciculture, as now understood and carried on, would be an unalloyed pleasure and unbounded success. We can practically hatch 995 out of 1,000 eggs, or thereabouts. It is the risks of rearing that stand in our road, and these, as time goes on, and experience increases, must diminish. There would appear, then, to be a good time coming for fish culture, and those who earnestly follow it.

Practice is the only safe guide, as circumstances, geological, physical, and meteorological so vary the conditions of works that no definite rule of procedure will avail. Earnest work and close observation, combined with ready resource, are the only safe guides to success. Troubles of some sort are sure to supervene; the man who succeeds is he who can anticipate, and so remedy them. To be always on the watch and notice the first indication is a very safe maxim, more easy to inculcate than to put in practice.

There can be no question but that the practical removal of difficulties in the path of fish culture is work of the highest value, well worthy the attention and acknowledgment of those in authority at Whitehall and elsewhere at home, as has been the case abroad.

C. C. C.

SIR,--Your correspondent "C. C. C." in *Land and Water* of last week disagrees with the constant and free use of earth, which I had advocated in my article on fish culture which appeared the preceding week. Naturally one must admit that earth at the bottom of a pond is not so great an element of beauty as is clean gravel, but the advantages are so many, that beauty must give way to usefulness. Besides this, "C. C. C." must know that it is almost impossible to keep the gravel clean enough to look pretty, when the water is inhabited by a large number of little fish which are being constantly fed. I cannot at all agree with his advice that "earth should be avoided, or only used when necessity dictates." I believe that one of the first principles of success in fish culture is always to prevent any disease or mishap, rather than to wait for, and then try to remedy it. Trout in their natural surroundings get a dose of earth every time that there is a spate. It is very evident that the earth contains some ingredients which are not only beneficial but almost a necessity to the fish.

I have never heard of earth as an actual cure for "fungus" and should hardly think that it is active enough. There is, however, no doubt that it is one of the best preventatives to "fungus," for if it is properly and freely used it stops all chance of any decomposing material being exposed to the action of the water, and laying the fish open to the chance of a great many evils.

If suitable earth is used once a week, and even oftener on occasions, it can do no harm, and will keep the fish safe from a great many risks besides doing them very material good. I do not of course mean that the usual weekly dose should be a large one, as this would fill up the pond before the end of the season, but that a small dose should be given generally, and a large dose occasionally. I am quite sure, too, that clean earth with some nice weeds growing in it, looks better than gravel which is dirty. Gravel shows the dirt so much, that it is almost impossible to keep it looking nice where there are many fish, and it also gives the water free access to any decomposing matter.

I have never come across a case of disease caused by the use of earth, and should like to hear the details of "C. C. C.'s" experiences with regard to this matter.

CHARLES WALKER.

INDEX

Butler & Tanner, The Selwood Printing Works, Frome, and London.

Shooting on a Small Income

By CHARLES WALKER

Illustrated. Crown 8vo, 5s.

"A pleasant little surprise awaited us when we found on our table ... 'Shooting on a Small Income.' The marked individuality of this book lies in the fact that in the course of 300 odd pages it gives in concise language an enormous body of information fully justifying the title chosen.... The amount of really useful all-round information presented in such a readable form would be almost impossible to beat in any single work that has come to our notice."--*Land and Water.*

On Plain and Peak

Sport in Bohemia and Tyrol

By RANDOLPH LLEWELLYN HODGSON

Illustrated by H.S.H. PRINCESS MARY OF THURN AND TAXIS, and from Photographs

Demy 8vo, 7*s*. 6*d*.

Days in Thule with Rod, Gun, and Camera

By JOHN BICKERDYKE

With Numerous Illustrations. Cloth, 2*s*. 6*d*.; paper cover, 1*s*. 6*d*.

Motor Vehicles and Motors

Their Design, Construction, and Working by Steam, Oil, and Electricity

By W. WORBY BEAUMONT

M.INST.C.E. M.INST.M.E. M.INST.E.E.

Price 42*s*. net

About six hundred pages and more than four hundred and fifty illustrations and working drawings.

The Eighth Duke of Beaufort

AND THE BADMINTON HUNT

With a Sketch of the Rise of the Somerset Family

By T. F. DALE, M.A.

AUTHOR OF "THE HISTORY OF THE BELVOIR HUNT," "THE GAME OF POLO," ETC.

Demy 8vo, 21*s*. Fully Illustrated.

The History of the Belvoir Hunt

By T. F. DALE, M.A.

With 5 Photogravures and 48 Full-page Plates, and 2 Maps of the Country hunted, showing all the principal meets and historic runs. Also Appendices giving the Stud Book Entries from the year 1791 to 1876, pedigrees of celebrated hounds, and a bibliography.

1 Vol. Demy 8vo. 21s. net

"Mr. Dale's book must be read through and through--by the sportsman for pleasure, the historian for facts, and by the breeders of all animals for the results of judicious mating. It is about the best work on a hunting subject ever written."--*Sporting Life.*

"He has produced a book which is much more than its title promises, and he has indeed been fortunate in his subject. While Mr. Dale's record centres upon the hunting field and kennel with scrupulous care for detail that hunt history demands, he invests it with stronger claims still upon attention."--*Bailey's Magazine.*

2 WHITEHALL GARDENS, WESTMINSTER

---

produced from images generously made available by The Internet Archive/American Libraries.)

Updated editions will replace the previous one--the old editions will be renamed.

Creating the works from public domain print editions means that no one owns a United States copyright in these works, so the Foundation (and you!) can copy and distribute it in the United States without permission and without paying copyright royalties. Special rules, set forth in the General Terms of Use part of this license, apply to copying and distributing Project Gutenberg-tm electronic works to protect the PROJECT GUTENBERG-tm concept and trademark. Project Gutenberg is a registered trademark, and may not be used if you charge for the eBooks, unless you receive specific permission. If you do not charge anything for copies of this eBook, complying with the rules is very easy. You may use this eBook for nearly any purpose such as creation of derivative works, reports, performances and research. They may be modified and printed and given away--you may do practically ANYTHING with public domain eBooks. Redistribution is subject to the trademark license, especially commercial redistribution.

*** START: FULL LICENSE ***

THE FULL PROJECT GUTENBERG LICENSE PLEASE READ THIS BEFORE YOU DISTRIBUTE OR USE THIS WORK

To protect the Project Gutenberg-tm mission of promoting the free distribution of electronic works, by using or distributing this work (or any other work associated in any way with the phrase "Project Gutenberg"), you agree to comply with all the terms of the Full Project Gutenberg-tm License (available with this file or online at http://gutenberg.org/license).

Section 1. General Terms of Use and Redistributing Project
Gutenberg-tm electronic works

1.A. By reading or using any part of this Project Gutenberg-tm
electronic work, you indicate that you have read, understand,
agree to and accept all the terms of this license and intellectual
property (trademark/copyright) agreement. If you do not agree to
abide by all the terms of this agreement, you must cease using
and return or destroy all copies of Project Gutenberg-tm
electronic works in your possession. If you paid a fee for
obtaining a copy of or access to a Project Gutenberg-tm
electronic work and you do not agree to be bound by the terms
of this agreement, you may obtain a refund from the person or
entity to whom you paid the fee as set forth in paragraph 1.E.8.

1.B. "Project Gutenberg" is a registered trademark. It may only
be used on or associated in any way with an electronic work by
people who agree to be bound by the terms of this agreement.
There are a few things that you can do with most Project
Gutenberg-tm electronic works even without complying with the
full terms of this agreement. See paragraph 1.C below. There
are a lot of things you can do with Project Gutenberg-tm
electronic works if you follow the terms of this agreement and
help preserve free future access to Project Gutenberg-tm
electronic works. See paragraph 1.E below.

1.C. The Project Gutenberg Literary Archive Foundation ("the
Foundation" or PGLAF), owns a compilation copyright in the
collection of Project Gutenberg-tm electronic works. Nearly all
the individual works in the collection are in the public domain in
the United States. If an individual work is in the public domain in
the United States and you are located in the United States, we
do not claim a right to prevent you from copying, distributing,
performing, displaying or creating derivative works based on the
work as long as all references to Project Gutenberg are
removed. Of course, we hope that you will support the Project

Gutenberg-tm mission of promoting free access to electronic works by freely sharing Project Gutenberg-tm works in compliance with the terms of this agreement for keeping the Project Gutenberg-tm name associated with the work. You can easily comply with the terms of this agreement by keeping this work in the same format with its attached full Project Gutenberg-tm License when you share it without charge with others.

1.D. The copyright laws of the place where you are located also govern what you can do with this work. Copyright laws in most countries are in a constant state of change. If you are outside the United States, check the laws of your country in addition to the terms of this agreement before downloading, copying, displaying, performing, distributing or creating derivative works based on this work or any other Project Gutenberg-tm work. The Foundation makes no representations concerning the copyright status of any work in any country outside the United States.

1.E. Unless you have removed all references to Project Gutenberg:

1.E.1. The following sentence, with active links to, or other immediate access to, the full Project Gutenberg-tm License must appear prominently whenever any copy of a Project Gutenberg-tm work (any work on which the phrase "Project Gutenberg" appears, or with which the phrase "Project Gutenberg" is associated) is accessed, displayed, performed, viewed, copied or distributed:

This eBook is for the use of anyone anywhere at no cost and with almost no restrictions whatsoever. You may copy it, give it away or re-use it under the terms of the Project Gutenberg License included with this eBook or online at www.gutenberg.org

1.E.2. If an individual Project Gutenberg-tm electronic work is derived from the public domain (does not contain a notice indicating that it is posted with permission of the copyright holder), the work can be copied and distributed to anyone in the United States without paying any fees or charges. If you are redistributing or providing access to a work with the phrase "Project Gutenberg" associated with or appearing on the work, you must comply either with the requirements of paragraphs 1.E.1 through 1.E.7 or obtain permission for the use of the work and the Project Gutenberg-tm trademark as set forth in paragraphs 1.E.8 or 1.E.9.

1.E.3. If an individual Project Gutenberg-tm electronic work is posted with the permission of the copyright holder, your use and distribution must comply with both paragraphs 1.E.1 through 1.E.7 and any additional terms imposed by the copyright holder. Additional terms will be linked to the Project Gutenberg-tm License for all works posted with the permission of the copyright holder found at the beginning of this work.

1.E.4. Do not unlink or detach or remove the full Project Gutenberg-tm License terms from this work, or any files containing a part of this work or any other work associated with Project Gutenberg-tm.

1.E.5. Do not copy, display, perform, distribute or redistribute this electronic work, or any part of this electronic work, without prominently displaying the sentence set forth in paragraph 1.E.1 with active links or immediate access to the full terms of the Project Gutenberg-tm License.

1.E.6. You may convert to and distribute this work in any binary, compressed, marked up, nonproprietary or proprietary form, including any word processing or hypertext form. However, if you provide access to or distribute copies of a Project Gutenberg-tm work in a format other than "Plain Vanilla ASCII" or other format used in the official version posted on the official Project Gutenberg-tm web site (www.gutenberg.org), you must, at no additional cost, fee or expense to the user, provide a copy, a means of exporting a copy, or a means of obtaining a copy upon request, of the work in its original "Plain Vanilla ASCII" or other form. Any alternate format must include the full Project Gutenberg-tm License as specified in paragraph 1.E.1.

1.E.7. Do not charge a fee for access to, viewing, displaying, performing, copying or distributing any Project Gutenberg-tm works unless you comply with paragraph 1.E.8 or 1.E.9.

1.E.8. You may charge a reasonable fee for copies of or providing access to or distributing Project Gutenberg-tm electronic works provided that

- You pay a royalty fee of 20% of the gross profits you derive from the use of Project Gutenberg-tm works calculated using the method you already use to calculate your applicable taxes. The fee is owed to the owner of the Project Gutenberg-tm trademark, but he has agreed to donate royalties under this paragraph to the Project Gutenberg Literary Archive Foundation. Royalty payments must be paid within 60 days following each date on which you prepare (or are legally required to prepare) your periodic tax returns. Royalty payments should be clearly marked as such and sent to the Project Gutenberg Literary Archive Foundation at the address specified in Section 4, "Information about donations to the Project Gutenberg Literary Archive Foundation."

- You provide a full refund of any money paid by a user who notifies you in writing (or by e-mail) within 30 days of receipt that s/he does not agree to the terms of the full Project Gutenberg-tm License. You must require such a user to return or destroy all copies of the works possessed in a physical medium and discontinue all use of and all access to other copies of Project

Gutenberg-tm works.

- You provide, in accordance with paragraph 1.F.3, a full refund of any money paid for a work or a replacement copy, if a defect in the electronic work is discovered and reported to you within 90 days of receipt of the work.

- You comply with all other terms of this agreement for free distribution of Project Gutenberg-tm works.

1.E.9. If you wish to charge a fee or distribute a Project Gutenberg-tm electronic work or group of works on different terms than are set forth in this agreement, you must obtain permission in writing from both the Project Gutenberg Literary Archive Foundation and Michael Hart, the owner of the Project Gutenberg-tm trademark. Contact the Foundation as set forth in Section 3 below.

1.F.

1.F.1. Project Gutenberg volunteers and employees expend considerable effort to identify, do copyright research on, transcribe and proofread public domain works in creating the Project Gutenberg-tm collection. Despite these efforts, Project Gutenberg-tm electronic works, and the medium on which they may be stored, may contain "Defects," such as, but not limited to, incomplete, inaccurate or corrupt data, transcription errors, a copyright or other intellectual property infringement, a defective or damaged disk or other medium, a computer virus, or computer codes that damage or cannot be read by your equipment.

1.F.2. LIMITED WARRANTY, DISCLAIMER OF DAMAGES - Except for the "Right of Replacement or Refund" described in paragraph 1.F.3, the Project Gutenberg Literary Archive Foundation, the owner of the Project Gutenberg-tm trademark, and any other party distributing a Project Gutenberg-tm electronic work under this agreement, disclaim all liability to you for damages, costs and expenses, including legal fees. YOU AGREE THAT YOU HAVE NO REMEDIES FOR NEGLIGENCE, STRICT LIABILITY, BREACH OF WARRANTY OR BREACH OF CONTRACT EXCEPT THOSE PROVIDED IN PARAGRAPH F3. YOU AGREE THAT THE FOUNDATION, THE TRADEMARK OWNER, AND ANY DISTRIBUTOR UNDER THIS AGREEMENT WILL NOT BE LIABLE TO YOU FOR ACTUAL, DIRECT, INDIRECT, CONSEQUENTIAL, PUNITIVE OR INCIDENTAL DAMAGES EVEN IF YOU GIVE NOTICE OF THE POSSIBILITY OF SUCH DAMAGE.

1.F.3. LIMITED RIGHT OF REPLACEMENT OR REFUND - If you discover a defect in this electronic work within 90 days of receiving it, you can receive a refund of the money (if any) you paid for it by sending a written explanation to the person you received the work from. If you received the work on a physical medium, you must return the medium with your written explanation. The person or entity that provided you with the defective work may elect to provide a replacement copy in lieu of a refund. If you received the work electronically, the person or entity providing it to you may choose to give you a second opportunity to receive the work electronically in lieu of a refund. If the second copy is also defective, you may demand a refund in writing without further opportunities to fix the problem.

1.F.4. Except for the limited right of replacement or refund set forth in paragraph 1.F.3, this work is provided to you 'AS-IS' WITH NO OTHER WARRANTIES OF ANY KIND, EXPRESS OR IMPLIED, INCLUDING BUT NOT LIMITED TO WARRANTIES OF MERCHANTIBILITY OR FITNESS FOR ANY PURPOSE.

1.F.5. Some states do not allow disclaimers of certain implied warranties or the exclusion or limitation of certain types of damages. If any disclaimer or limitation set forth in this agreement violates the law of the state applicable to this agreement, the agreement shall be interpreted to make the maximum disclaimer or limitation permitted by the applicable state law. The invalidity or unenforceability of any provision of this agreement shall not void the remaining provisions.

1.F.6. **INDEMNITY**

- You agree to indemnify and hold the Foundation, the trademark owner, any agent or employee of the Foundation, anyone providing copies of Project Gutenberg-tm electronic works in accordance with this agreement, and any volunteers associated with the production, promotion and distribution of Project Gutenberg-tm electronic works, harmless from all liability, costs and expenses, including legal fees, that arise directly or indirectly from any of the following which you do or cause to occur: (a) distribution of this or any Project Gutenberg-tm work, (b) alteration, modification, or additions or deletions to any Project Gutenberg-tm work, and (c) any Defect you cause.

Section 2. Information about the Mission of Project Gutenberg-tm

Project Gutenberg-tm is synonymous with the free distribution of electronic works in formats readable by the widest variety of computers including obsolete, old, middle-aged and new computers. It exists because of the efforts of hundreds of volunteers and donations from people in all walks of life.

Volunteers and financial support to provide volunteers with the assistance they need, is critical to reaching Project Gutenberg-tm's goals and ensuring that the Project Gutenberg-tm collection will remain freely available for generations to come. In 2001, the Project Gutenberg Literary Archive Foundation was created to provide a secure and permanent future for Project Gutenberg-tm and future generations. To learn more about the Project Gutenberg Literary Archive Foundation and how your efforts and donations can

help, see Sections 3 and 4 and the Foundation web page at
http://www.pglaf.org.

Section 3. Information about the Project Gutenberg Literary
Archive Foundation

The Project Gutenberg Literary Archive Foundation is a non
profit 501(c)(3) educational corporation organized under the laws
of the state of Mississippi and granted tax exempt status by the
Internal Revenue Service. The Foundation's EIN or federal tax
identification number is 64-6221541. Its 501(c)(3) letter is posted
at http://pglaf.org/fundraising. Contributions to the Project
Gutenberg Literary Archive Foundation are tax deductible to the
full extent permitted by U.S. federal laws and your state's laws.

The Foundation's principal office is located at 4557 Melan Dr. S.
Fairbanks, AK, 99712., but its volunteers and employees are
scattered throughout numerous locations. Its business office is
located at 809 North 1500 West, Salt Lake City, UT 84116, (801)
596-1887, email business@pglaf.org. Email contact links and up
to date contact information can be found at the Foundation's web
site and official page at http://pglaf.org

For additional contact information: Dr. Gregory B. Newby Chief
Executive and Director gbnewby@pglaf.org

Section 4. Information about Donations to the Project Gutenberg
Literary Archive Foundation

Project Gutenberg-tm depends upon and cannot survive without
wide spread public support and donations to carry out its mission
of increasing the number of public domain and licensed works
that can be freely distributed in machine readable form
accessible by the widest array of equipment including outdated
equipment. Many small donations ($1 to $5,000) are particularly
important to maintaining tax exempt status with the IRS.

The Foundation is committed to complying with the laws regulating charities and charitable donations in all 50 states of the United States. Compliance requirements are not uniform and it takes a considerable effort, much paperwork and many fees to meet and keep up with these requirements. We do not solicit donations in locations where we have not received written confirmation of compliance. To SEND DONATIONS or determine the status of compliance for any particular state visit http://pglaf.org

While we cannot and do not solicit contributions from states where we have not met the solicitation requirements, we know of no prohibition against accepting unsolicited donations from donors in such states who approach us with offers to donate.

International donations are gratefully accepted, but we cannot make any statements concerning tax treatment of donations received from outside the United States. U.S. laws alone swamp our small staff.

Please check the Project Gutenberg Web pages for current donation methods and addresses. Donations are accepted in a number of other ways including checks, online payments and credit card donations. To donate, please visit: http://pglaf.org/donate

Section 5. General Information About Project Gutenberg-tm electronic works.

Professor Michael S. Hart is the originator of the Project Gutenberg-tm concept of a library of electronic works that could be freely shared with anyone. For thirty years, he produced and distributed Project Gutenberg-tm eBooks with only a loose network of volunteer support.

Fish Culture, by Charles Edward Walker